SUPER SUMMER ACTIVITY BOOK

by Gabriella DeGennaro

illustrated by Scott Brooks

FIND THE SHADES

We're turning up the heat with our first sizzling summer challenge! Phil and Phyllis wear some sweet shades in this book. How many pictures of them wearing sunglasses can you find on the activity pages of this book?

Write your answer here: _____

MAD LIBS

An imprint of Penguin Random House LLC, New York

First published in the United States of America by Mad Libs,
an imprint of Penguin Random House LLC, New York, 2023

Mad Libs format and text copyright © 2023 by Penguin Random House LLC

Concept created by Roger Price & Leonard Stern

Designed by Dinardo Design

Visit us online at penguinrandomhouse.com.

Manufactured in China

ISBN 9780593523216

3 5 7 9 10 8 6 4 2

HH

RIDICULOUSLY SIMPLE INSTRUCTIONS

Mad Libs is an amazing way to create your own hysterically funny stories! To play, fill in the blanks with different types of words, like nouns, adjectives, or even exclamations. In case you've forgotten what nouns, adjectives, and verbs are, here is a quick review:

A **NOUN** is the name of a person, place, or thing. *Toaster*, *umbrella*, *bathtub*, and *pillow* are nouns. A Mad Libs will sometimes ask for a specific type of noun, like an **ANIMAL** (*tiger*), **ARTICLE OF CLOTHING** (*glove*), **OCCUPATION** (*astronaut*), or **CELEBRITY** (*Abraham Lincoln*). When a Mad Libs asks for **A PLACE**, it means any location (*Africa*, *barbershop*, *kitchen*, or *coral reef*).

An **ADJECTIVE** describes something or someone. *Lumpy*, *soft*, *pretty*, *messy*, and *tall* are adjectives. A Mad Libs will sometimes ask for a specific type of adjective, like a **COLOR** (*blue*).

A **VERB** is an action word. *Eat*, *sculpt*, and *collect* are verbs. A Mad Libs will sometimes ask for a **VERB ENDING IN "S"** (*runs*), a **VERB ENDING IN "ING"** (*pitching*), or a **VERB (PAST TENSE)** (*jumped* or *swam*).

An **EXCLAMATION** is anything a person or other creature would say, like *hey!*, *wow!*, *ouch!*, *meow!*, or *yikes!* **A SILLY WORD** is any made-up word or a word that just sounds funny, like *ooopatoopa!*, *squipple!*, or *whammo!* **A SOUND** is any noise, like *boing!*, *ding!*, *grunt!*, or *screech!*

When a Mad Libs asks for a **PLURAL**, it means more than one. For example, the plural of *cat* is *cats*.

When a Mad Libs asks for the **SAME** type of word, write in the same word you chose earlier in the story. For example, if you chose *chair* as a **NOUN** earlier in the story, you would write *chair* again for the **SAME NOUN**.

All Packed Up and Ready to...

Phil is going on summer vacation, but he hasn't packed yet. Help Phil complete his packing list by filling out the Mad Libs below.

Phil's Packing List

☐ Tooth-_____
　　　　　NOUN

☐ _____-paste
　PART OF THE BODY

☐ Six pairs of clean _____
　　　　　　　　　PLURAL NOUN

☐ _____ polka-dot _____
　COLOR　　　　　　　　　ARTICLE OF CLOTHING

☐ _____ , my favorite stuffed _____
　CELEBRITY　　　　　　　　　　　ANIMAL

☐ Denim _____
　　　　PLURAL NOUN

☐ _____ phone charger
　NOUN

☐ _____ pairs of _____ socks
　NUMBER　　　　　　ADJECTIVE

☐ _____-flops
　SILLY WORD

Use the stickers in the back of this book to fill up Phil's suitcase.

BONUS CHALLENGE:
Fill in the blanks using only words that begin with the letter *B*. Have fun! There are no wrong answers!

3

Phyllis's Way or the _____-way

ADJECTIVE

Phyllis needs help getting to the beach. To help her, unscramble the street names. Then, put an arrow sticker on the street names that are adjectives to show Phyllis the right way to go. _____ luck!

ADJECTIVE

PMRUETT

_ _ _ _ _ M _ _ E _ _   STREET

TAWSEY

_ _ _ _ _ A _ _ _ Y AVENUE

PYAHP

_ _ _ _ _ P _ _ WAY

TPEPPU

_ _ _ _ _ P _ _ T ROAD

OSTL

_ _ _ _ T WAY

4

IERST

_____ E ___ AVENUE

VYRCU

___ R _____ COURT

RVDIRE

__ R _____ R ROAD

RPEUS

_____ E ___ STREET

ERPIPYSL

__ L __ P __ E ____ STREET

Words Must Be This Tall!

This roller coaster has it all: twists, loops, and huge _____ ! But

PLURAL NOUN

let's see which words are tall enough to ride. Starting at the bottom of the

page, fill in the blanks with words that have seven or more letters. Words with

fewer than seven letters are too short!

10
9
8
7
6
5
4
3
2
1

N
R
O
C
P
O
P

YOU
MUST
BE THIS
TALL TO
RIDE

Start your word in the bottom box.

6

Ride the Tongue Twister

Are you ready to ride the Tongue Twister? _____!
EXCLAMATION

Fill in the blanks with words that start with *T* to finish the tongue

twister below, then recite them as fast as you can. How many times

can you say the tongue twister before *you* get tongue-tied?

Ten tangerines _____ twelve jelly beans
VERB (PAST TENSE) THAT STARTS WITH *T*

till they tumbled to _____ on Tuesday.
A PLACE THAT STARTS WITH *T*

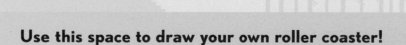

Use this space to draw your own roller coaster!

I Scream, You _____ !

We all scream for ice _____ ! Create your own ice cream by using

the Mad Libs Flavor Generator! To use the generator, fill in

the flavors from the list below that start with the same

letter of the alphabet as your answers on page 9.

FLAVOR GENERATOR

Apple

Bacon

Cherry

Doughnut

Eggplant

French fry

Gummy bear

Ham

Iceberg lettuce

Jelly beans

Kiwi

Lime

Mushrooms

Noodles

Olive

Peanuts

Quesadilla

Ramen

Sushi

Tortilla

Upside-down cake

Vanilla bean

Watermelon

X-mas cookie

Yolk

Zucchini

FLAVOR 1: Cookies and _____

FLAVOR THAT STARTS WITH FIRST LETTER OF YOUR NAME

FLAVOR 2: Double _____ Swirl

FLAVOR THAT STARTS WITH FIRST LETTER OF YOUR FAVORITE COLOR

FLAVOR 3: _____ Chip

FLAVOR THAT STARTS WITH FIRST LETTER OF YOUR FAVORITE ANIMAL

FLAVOR 4: _____ Cookie Dough

FLAVOR THAT STARTS WITH LAST LETTER OF YOUR FIRST NAME

FLAVOR 5: Rocky _____

FLAVOR THAT STARTS WITH FIRST LETTER OF YOUR FAVORITE BOOK

Now pick your *favorite* new flavor and draw it below. You can decorate your flavor with the delicious topping stickers in the back of this book!

MY FAVORITE FLAVOR IS: _____

Letter from Space Camp

Dear _____,
       FIRST NAME

Do you want to know all about how _____ camp
                                          NOUN

is going for me? Spoiler alert: It's _____! Here at
                                         ADJECTIVE

_____ -A- _____ -A Headquarters,
LETTER OF THE ALPHABET   LETTER OF THE ALPHABET

I'm learning about becoming a/an _____ who will
                                      OCCUPATION

one day _____ in outer space! I even learned how to
              VERB

steer my very own space-_____. This is so much
                              VEHICLE

better than _____ -ball camp! Last year at this time,
              PART OF THE BODY

I was _____ touchdowns, and this year I built a robot
      VERB ENDING IN "ING"

called the _____ -inator _____. I heard
                NOUN   NUMBER

_____ is interested in buying it! Can you believe
  CELEBRITY

what a great _____ I'm having at camp? Mom and
                  NOUN

_____ are so _____, they even sent me my
  CELEBRITY   ADJECTIVE

own space _____ and a/an _____ full of
           ARTICLE OF CLOTHING   TYPE OF CONTAINER

_____ shaped like the _____ planets in the
  TYPE OF FOOD   NUMBER

solar system.

        Your _____ friend,
                  ADJECTIVE

        _____
           YOUR NAME

Decorate this letter with outer space stickers from the back of this book!

P in the Pool!

The pool is full of *P*... words. Find all the *P* words in the pool and use the **secret clue** below to find out who put all the *P* in the pool.

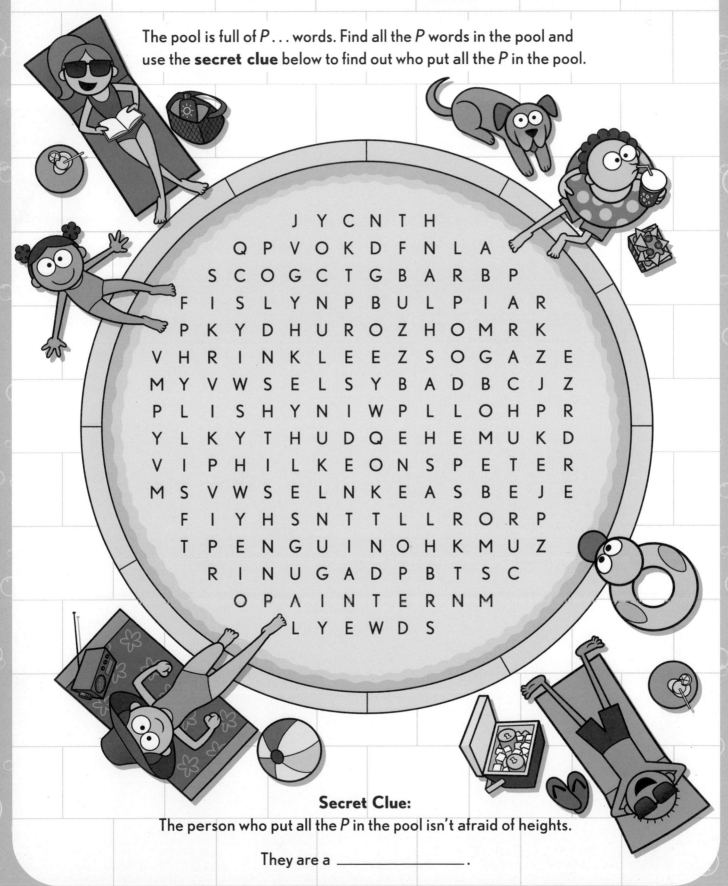

```
    J Y C N T H
  Q P V O K D F N L A
  S C O G C T G B A R B P
F I S L Y N P B U L P I A R
P K Y D H U R O Z H O M R K
V H R I N K L E E Z S O G A Z E
M Y V W S E L S Y B A D B C J Z
P L I S H Y N I W P L L O H P R
Y L K Y T H U D Q E H E M U K D
V I P H I L K E O N S P E T E R
M S V W S E L N K E A S B E J E
F I Y H S N T T L L R O R P
T P E N G U I N O H K M U Z
R I N U G A D P B T S C
  O P A I N T E R N M
    L Y E W D S
```

Secret Clue:
The person who put all the *P* in the pool isn't afraid of heights.

They are a _____ .

11

Hot Dog Contest

Step right up! Phil and Phyllis made hot dogs for the fair. In each column, write a noun or verb that starts with the letter *H* on their hot dogs. The column with the most words wins!

NOUN HOT DOGS

VERB HOT DOGS

Use the stickers in the back of this book to give a prize to the winning hot dog!

Summer Rules!

Just in time for summer vacation, Phil has posted some new rules on his door! Complete the rules below. Then, use the stickers in the back of this book to decorate Phil's door!

Phil's Summer Rules

1. No entry before _____ o'clock!
   NUMBER

2. No little _____ !
   OCCUPATION (PLURAL)

3. No _____ or _____ -wheeling in my room!
   VERB ENDING IN "ING"   NOUN

4. No _____ music!
   ADJECTIVE

5. Daylight _____ my _____ !
   VERB ENDING IN "S"   PART OF THE BODY (PLURAL)

6. Leave _____ by the door and step away!
   TYPE OF FOOD (PLURAL)

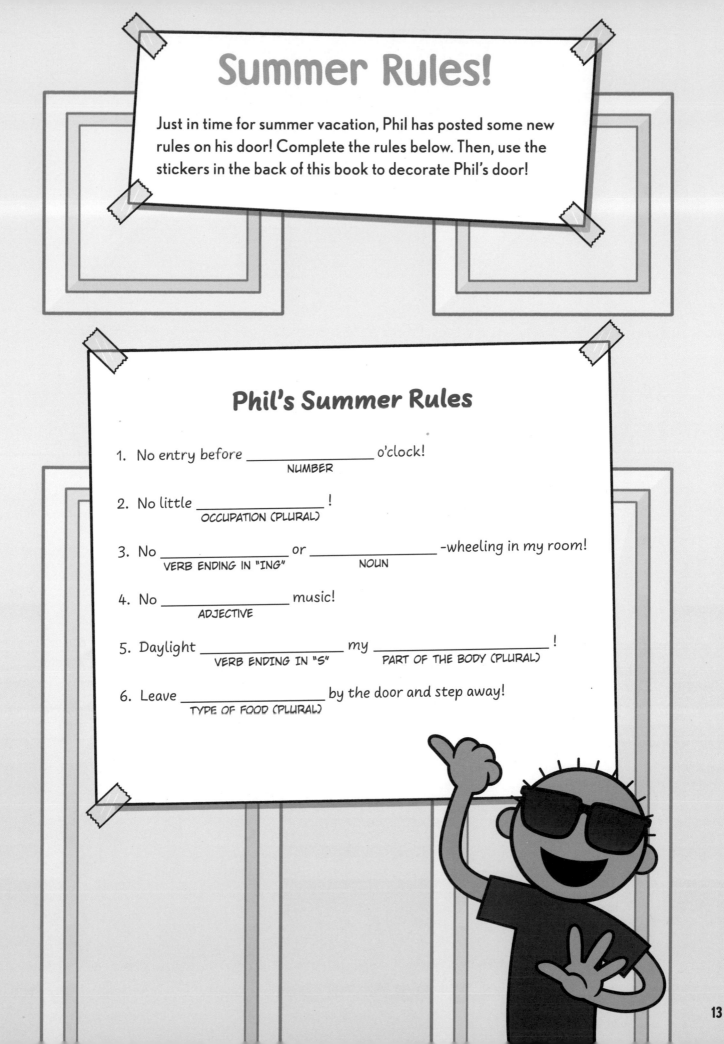

Time to Climb!

Phil wants to climb the rock wall. Help him find his way up by unscrambling the words on each path!

Once you've unscrambled as many words as you can, draw your own flag to put at the top of the rock wall.

DIFFICULTY KEY:
Green: You got this!
Yellow: Don't look down!
Red: Super difficult climb!

_ _ _ _ _ _ _ _ _
saveserc

_ _ _ _ _ _ _ _ _
nusneresc

_ _ _ _ _   _ _ _ _ _ _ _
owloly   momtham

_ _ _ _ _ _ _ _ _ _
ratzinggas

_ _ _ _ _ _ _
dodorew

_ _ _ _ _ _
gipoen

_ _ _ _ _ _ _
gibfoto

_ _ _ _ _ _ _   _ _ _ _ _
ublored   lgeea

_ _ _ _ _ _   _ _ _ _ _
lehmet   tosob

_ _ _ _ _   _ _ _ _
dioar   epor

_ _ _ _ _   _ _ _ _ _
uyddm   nunsy

_ _ _ _
erab

_ _ _ _
ampc

15

Answer Key

Page 1

Phil and Phyllis wear sunglasses **11** times on the activity pages of this book. They are on pages 3, 4, 7, 8, 11, 12, 13, and 15.

Pages 4–5

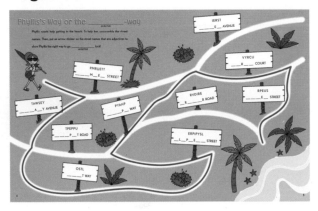

Page 4: Trumpet Street, Sweaty Avenue, Happy Way, Puppet Road, Lost Way

Page 5: Tires Avenue, Curvy Court, Driver Road, Super Street, Slippery Street

Page 11

Words from the word finder: painter, parachuter, Penelope, penguin, Peter, Phil, Phyllis, poodle, president

Secret Clue: The person who put all the *P* in the pool isn't afraid of heights. They are a parachuter.

Page 14

Green path:
camp (ampc), bear (erab), sunny (nunsy), rope (epor), boots (tosob), eagle (lgeea)

Yellow path:
muddy (uyddm), radio (dioar), helmet (lehmet), boulder (ublored), bigfoot (gibfoto), pigeon (gipoen)

Red path:
redwood (dodorew), stargazing (ratzinggas), woolly mammoth (owloly momtham), sunscreen (nusneresc), crevasse (saveserc)

Use these stickers on page 3

Use these stickers on pages 4–5

Use these stickers on page 9

Use these stickers on page 10

Use these stickers on page 12

Use these stickers on page 13

DANGER
KEEP OUT

GAMER
AT WORK

LEAVE
FOOD & DRINK
BY DOOR

WARNING

Bonus Stickers!